JEFFREY R. FIDEL, MD

The purpose of this book is to educate. It is not intended to serve as a replacement for professional medical advice. Any use of the information in this book is at the reader's discretion. This book is sold with the understanding that the author has no liability or responsibility for any injury caused or alleged to be caused directly or indirectly by the information contained in this book. The book's contents should not be construed as medical advice. To obtain medical advice on your individual health needs, please consult a qualified health care practitioner.

ISBN: 978-0-69277-265-2

Cover art: Jeffrey R. Fidel, MD
Design & layout: Gary A. Rosenberg • www.thebookcouple.com
Editor: Dina L. Wilcox

Printed in the United States of America

To my son, Andrew

eternity

you were always there

you were never born

you will never die

My mind gave you the name "heart"
but you are nameless
eternally beating

with or without me

Contents

Preface xiii

The Meaning of the Title xv

Why the Book xvii

The Arrangement of the Book xix

SECTION ONE **I MYSELF**

Who Am I? 3

My Mind's Creation of My Egoic Self 5

My Awakening 8

Not My First Time 10

My "Shrink" 13

My Decision to Stop the Medications 15

My Request 18

Entrance to the Door Within Myself 20

Not Since My Childhood 23

My Solo Journey Inward 25

My "Out-of-Body" Experience 27

My Mind's Conversation with God 29

My Obsessive-Compulsive Behavior 32

My Insight 34

My Act of Forgiveness 36

My Mind Becomes Aware of the Voice
      from My Heart 38

My Ego Reasserts Itself 42

My Cosmic Body 45

My Search for I Has Ended .47

SECTION TWO   I AS NON-DUAL I (ONE)

The World of Non-Duality 51

Non-Duality as a State of Awareness 52

The Reductive (Dual) Nature of Labels
      and Symbols for "Things" 53

The Reductive (Dual) Nature of Labels
      and Symbols for "Humans" 55

The Observable (and Non-Observable)
      Universe as a Reflection of Ourselves 57

Science as the Creation of Dualities 59

Thought and Sense Perceptions Creating
      Dualities 60

Scientific Proof We and the Universe
      Are One 62

True Self as the Non-Dual State of Self 64

Ego as the Dual State of Self 65

Subtle and Non-Subtle Forms of
a "Tornado" 66

Subtle and Non-Subtle Forms of
"I" Myself 67

Knowledge of Self Through Consciousness 68

Ego as the Creation of a Self by Thought-
Observation 69

The Scientific Dualistic Perception of
the Universe 70

The Rise of the Non-Dual Universe
Becoming Aware of Its Consciousness 71

Acknowledgments 73

References 75

About the Author 77

destiny

before my heart had a name
before its first flicker
it was already there.
it already knew

Implantation

Alas

the seed is sewn

the hunger is for nourishment
reaching beyond itself
implanting into the lush new supply
sinking deep into the soil of the womb
the seed is planted

Preface

I am not favoring any belief system.

I am not recommending any course of action.

I am not approving or condemning any way of living.

—J.R.F.M.D.

I(1) *for all and all for* I(1)
all is I(1)
I(Myself) *am a part of this* I(1)

The Meaning of the Title

The title of this book, **I**, is simply a symbol. It is a single vertical line.

This line can represent many different things, depending on the mind of the interpreter and the context in which it is presented.

For the purposes of this book, this vertical line is a symbol representing I(Myself) and I(One).

What is most important is that I is a symbol.

A symbol does not represent the true essence of what is being represented.

A symbol (name) reduces true essence into just that, a symbol (name).

True essence is unnamable.

No destination

Happiness is a state of mind
Inner Peace is a state of being

Why the Book

This book describes my awakening, which occurred when I lost my marriage and my beloved dog, Teenie, and when I voluntarily left my professional career as a practicing medical doctor.

It was also at this time that I made the deeply personal decision to stop taking my medications for bipolar I disorder.

My sense of self during this time had been largely dependent upon these components, which resided outside of me.

When these components fell away, "I" was all that was left.

At the time, "I" had been a compilation of acquired ideas in my mind and, therefore, had little-to-no sense of being.

It is

It is what it is

The Arrangement of the Book

This book, I, is arranged into two main sections:

Section One is the I(Myself) telling the story of my personal awakening.

Section Two is the I, meaning the "*one*ness" of all existence (i.e., non-duality).

the vow

I, __ self__, take you, __ self __, to be myself.

I promise to be true to you in good times
and in bad, in sickness and in health.

I will love you and honor you
all the days of my life.

SECTION ONE

I MYSELF

Who Am I?

I(My Being, or essence, which includes my mind) am intrinsically unknowable by my mind, because I cannot be reconstructed with collections of thoughts, words, or beliefs.

I(My Being, or essence), therefore, cannot be reduced to words like "I" or "self"; nor can my acquired belief system reconstruct or explain my Being.

I(My Being, or essence) am woven into the Being, or essence, of the Universe, and therefore, I and the Universe are one.

I(My mind) am the awareness of the intrinsically unknowable and unnamable essence.

I(My mind) am aware that the voice from my heart is the voice of the Universe (essence) that **I(My Being, or essence)** am woven into.

ego heart

once shackled within the core of my being
under the control of my subconscious mind

lay a soulless muscle

in my mind's eye lay four chambers
filled with red oozing liquid
connected by opening and closing gates

mechanically pumping away...

My Mind's Creation
of My Egoic Self

I(My Being, or essence, which includes my mind) is, always was, and will always be my ever-changing, true identity.

As my Being grew up, it began to acquire (from society) a collection of ideas within its mind. This would turn out to be my lifelong creation of my mind's thought-based identity (egoic self). This egoic self began to identify itself as an "I," "Homo sapiens," "Male," "Jeffrey," "Born in New York," etc.

As life continued, my Being's mind stored and created more ideas. The societally acquired name "I" that is stored in my mind believed myself to be an "intelligent and diligent physician," an "animal lover," a "piano player," a "snow skier," a "husband," and a "father," etc.

I(My mind) believed that becoming better at these activities would "make me happy." In the end, though, none of these activities, by themselves, would complete the Being that I am. I(My mind) thought that it had "made it" on the outside by achieving high levels of expertise in these various activities.

Additionally, my mind acquired various beliefs on how to act. For example, my mind acquired the belief that it was not acceptable to cry in public. This created a conflict within my mind every time I wanted to cry. In order to compensate for this conflict, my mind repressed the rest of my being from carrying out its once-natural response. Over time, I(My mind) lost awareness of my Being, or essence. My mind's thoughts of who "I" was had taken over the unnamable "I"(My Being, or essence, which also includes the essence of my mind), of who "I" really was.

the largest?

*It would be egotistical to say
that I once had the largest ego*

My Awakening

It was not until the circumstances of my life crisis that I(My Being) began to wake up from the illusion of my mind's acquired thought-based life.

My Being had become all but lost.

My mind was never satisfied, since it existed solely as a collection of beliefs and ideas of what "I" should be, not the natural Being that "I" truly was.

Since my egoic self was an identity that consisted solely as a collection of ideas stored in my mind, it could never be fulfilled. My egoic self acquired a life of its own in a quest to define itself, by acquiring more and more ideas. In doing so, it began to lose awareness of its being.

My state of awakening occurred when my ego lost its power and, therefore, no longer dominated my Being.

My awakening occurred when the non-acquired thoughts from my heart, and the acquired thoughts from society, became two incompatible sets of thoughts within my mind.

a fool

*is it not foolish to think
you can fool yourself?*

Not My First Time

This was not the first time that my mind had created a major personal crisis in my life. My mind had created a similar situation about 15 years prior to my awakening, as I(My Being) had neared the end of my formal training as an allopathic physician specializing in the field of diagnostic radiology.

My mind had never accepted its fate to become a physician. My mind, therefore, generated a great amount of conflicting thoughts on completing my residency.

In order to protect my mind-based thought-created identity from its own "self-destructive" thoughts, I(My Being) subconsciously trained my mind to stop thinking.

My mind became like an on-off switch.

When my mind was "on," it was consumed by continuous thoughts of worthlessness. Since my identity was egoic at this time, my "depressed" thoughts resulted in my mind's creation of a belief of being depressed and, therefore, I(My mind) became depressed. I(My mind) was in a state labeled "depression."

When my mind was "off," it entered a state of mind-lessness. I(My mind), therefore, was "happy," since I(My mind) no longer had thoughts of worthlessness. Without competing thoughts within my mind, I(My mind) was also able to experience pure sensory awareness of the outside environment. I(My Being) walked around in a mental state of Nirvana, with my thoughtless mind providing me heightened perceptions of the physical senses of sight, hearing, taste, touch, and smell. I(My mind) had truly believed that the Universe had revealed itself. I(My mind) was in a state labeled "mania."

In my mind, I had become "enlightened." My mind thought, to itself, that it had finally found the answers to the problems of the world ("delusional").

I(My mind) was completely unaware that all it had created was its own escape drug.

My mentally created state of Nirvana scared people, since it was a radical deviation from what they had come to expect from me. All their (their minds') prior experiences with my former (mind-created) persona had led them to have societal expectations of acceptable behavior.

Knowledge

Knowledge is knowing it's unknowable

My "Shrink"

The psychiatrist I(My Being) presented myself to had his(His mind's) own ideas of what was "wrong with me," primarily because his mind was taught to believe in a guide that psychiatrists often refer to when they formulate their diagnoses. It is called the *Diagnostic and Statistical Manual of Mental Disorders (DSM)*.

He(His mind) labeled me(My Being, which includes my mind) "delusional" and "manic." Since he also elicited the history that I had formerly suffered bouts of "depression," I now "fit perfectly" into the *DSM* diagnostic label of "Bipolar I."

I(My Being) was initially placed on antipsychotic drugs and continued to take mood-stabilizing and antidepressant medications. I referred to my medications as my "chemical lobotomy." They enabled me to continue to "fit into" society, both as an individual and as a practicing physician. However, my mind's conflicting thoughts of becoming a practicing physician were never confronted; they were simply masked by the medications.

the past is the past

let the past be thy teacher,
not thy master

My Decision
to Stop the Medications

Shortly after my awakening, I became convinced that I was not a "bipolar type I." I believed this was a label given to me by society. How could I possibly be understood in a single short visit to a doctor's office?

I decided to stop taking my medications. I had been informed that I would probably be on these medications for the rest of my life, and I was no longer willing to accept that fate. I believed the medications took away my ability to be loving and compassionate, both to myself and to others. In short, they took away my humanity.

I knew it was a potentially dangerous decision to stop taking the medications, so I began my preparation by reading many books about the effects of withdrawal from medications. As expected, I did have withdrawals, at times severe, along with mental and physical sensations of agitation.

At times, I felt as if my brain was being ripped to pieces. Under ordinary circumstances, I would have been too scared to continue, but now I decided to allow myself to experience fully and embrace the sensations that were occurring in my head. I refused to label my experiences "painful" or "unusual."

This type of *meditation* became my new *medication*.

humility

humility is equality

"self" and "other" are concepts of the mind
Our hearts know that "We are One"

My Request

In an attempt to increase the safety of my journey, I sought the assistance of a "holistic" psychologist. I requested he observe me while I continued, slowly, tapering myself off the medications.

When I presented myself at his office, the psychologist became concerned. After our brief encounter, he rendered his decision. In his professional opinion, based on our brief interview, he did not believe I was of sound mind. He refused to play the role of observer, but he was willing to be an active participant by helping me "get better."

I felt his suggestion would be a hindrance to my journey to live my life medication-free. I made my decision and told him, "Thank you, but no thank you," and I walked away. I continued my slow tapering off of the medications.

In my mind, the only way I could continue my journey was by distancing myself from everyone and anyone around me who would not support my decision to take myself off the medications. In the end, I was, virtually, completely isolated.

closed mind/open heart

my mind wants it for me
my heart wants it for all;
I listen to my heart

Entrance to the Door Within Myself

For my mind to learn the Being of who I truly was, my mind would need to reconnect to the "inside of myself," where my Being resides: my heart.

How then to go inward?

This next phase of my journey included a course that employed the use of psychodrama. Psychodrama is a technique utilized to reenact past traumatic events in one's life. The course enabled me to do what I had not been able to do for a long time: reconnect with myself.

Before this course, I had only been involved with talk therapy. There, my ego would consciously, or subconsciously, defend itself, typically by assigning blame to someone or something outside of me.

For example, I had unresolved anger issues that stemmed from my belief that I was living my life to obtain approval from others, rather than living my life for myself.

By not taking complete responsibility for how I lived my life, I was never able to address my anger directly.

During the psychodrama course, I allowed myself to become vulnerable. I started to understand that "speaking" my past was different from experiencing my past. In the course, I allowed myself to feel—not with my mind, but with my entire being—the sensations that pulsated throughout my body as I poured my heart and soul out, just as if I was living in the past. Intense rage and tears usually accompanied each reenactment.

This was my first glimpse of true inner healing.

self-instruction manual

please look inside yourself before using

Not Since My Childhood

I became aware that this was the first time, since I was a child, that I allowed myself to feel. My subconscious fear of feeling had been prohibiting me from knowing myself. If I had felt discomfort in the past, I, consciously or subconsciously, reached for some*thing* or some activity (the medications, alcohol, sex, sky diving, etc.) to take away the unpleasant feeling.

It was during the psychodrama course that I had my first glimpse of reconnecting with something outside of my mind, and that was my heart. Between the defense mechanisms of my ego and the psychiatric medications that had numbed me, this was the first time I was actually aware of feeling my heart pulsating within me. I knew, at this point, that I would have to continue my journey inward, no matter where it would take me. Somehow, my heart knew the truth. It knew something my mind did not.

ego to ego

what did one ego say to the other?

*Nothing, (since) the ego knew the answer
before the question was asked.*

My Solo Journey Inward

I continued my journey inward for many months, mainly by utilizing Eastern instruction guides such as Lao Tzu's *Tao Te Ching* and *Hua Hu Ching*. These are how-to guides to achieving oneness with the unnamable Tao (Universe, God, etc.) through self-purification and self-mastery.

During this time, I abstained from all activities that I perceived to be desire- or fear-based, or somehow involved in the killing of living things. For me, this meant abstaining from sex, pornography, alcohol, and meat-eating.

Unknowingly, I had substituted one desire for another desire. What I was now desiring was "enlightenment."

The more I believed myself to be "spiritually advanced," the more intolerant I became of anyone I felt could not understand me.

I had unconsciously re-created a new mental/spiritual drug: the belief of spiritual advancement. As a result, I would endure immense suffering for the next few months that followed.

father to son

Dear Son,

You are whole and pure

Trust yourself

Be yourself

I am here for you

Love,
Dad

My "Out-of-Body" Experience

Slowly and subconsciously, over the months, I became so "mind-identified" (i.e., my mind predominately served as both my identity and reality at this time) that I had to rub my feet vigorously for my mind to retain awareness of its body(Being).

One night, when I was lying in bed, I(My mind) inadvertently shifted so much attention away from my body that I had the mental sensation of energy "tearing away" from my body. My mind lost its motor control of my body and retained only a vague, general somatic proprioception (body awareness). With my body lying inert on the bed, my mind created a vision of my son. I(My mind) realized I needed my body to be present for my son and, immediately, my mind's attention was directed back into my inert body.

As my mind's awareness of my body returned, I had the mental sensation of energy rapidly "refilling" my body, until my body was back under the full awareness of my mind and able to move again.

coming to senses

seeing is believing with your eyes
being is believing with your heart

My Mind's Conversation with God

Several days after my mind's perceived "out-of-body experience," I was called to the beach at four o'clock in the morning by my mind's own thought-created version of God.

Although I had been brought up under the religious faith of Judaism, I had never believed in God.

I got in my car and drove 15 minutes to the ocean. It was there that I was to have my mind-created conversation with God.

To be more precise, I yelled God's name ("AHHHHHHH") at the top of my lungs for hours. In my mind's eye, the clouds aligned themselves in waves across the sky, in what I perceived to be alignment with the vibrational frequency of my voice. A new city of clouds appeared on the horizon before me.

Although this was my own mental creation at the time, this God was completely real to me. This God who I was speaking to was humble, loving, truthful, courageous, and forgiving. I pledged my life to this God and promised to be a messenger.

However, whenever my mind failed to live up to its preconceived expectation of being "perfect," my mind would doubt the forgiving nature of its own mentally created God. At these times of perceived failure, I(My mind) thought that I(again, My mind, which was my entire sense of self at the time) would be put to death by a now vengeful God.

perfect illusion

There is no perfect without imperfect

My Obsessive-Compulsive Behavior

For the next few weeks, I compulsively checked the *I Ching* (the "Book of Changes," another spiritual guide to enlightenment) to insure that I remained sufficiently virtuous to deserve the role of God's messenger.

The *I Ching* is composed of 64 hexagrams.

The book can be said to be "dynamic," because it is the casting of coins that determines which hexagram one should consult.

I(My mind) interpreted the advice given by each hexagram as coming directly from God.

I began to scrutinize everything I did.

I continued to believe that I needed to be perfect.

mind your heart

forget with your mind
forgive with your heart
lead with your heart
let your mind follow

My Insight

By recalling some of my long-ago psychiatric interviews, I was able to make the correlation between my perception that I needed to be "perfect" to gain love and approval from my parents and my mental creation of God.

I left myself numerous reminder notes around my house that would serve as the lifeline between my internal dreamlike mind-created reality (my mental creation of God, based on the perception that I needed to be "perfect") and my external sensory-based perception of the world around me.

the first beat

I(My mind) do not recall
However, I(My mind) know it to be perfect:
the heart before my mind ever knew it
beating naturally to the rhythm of the soul
supplying
receiving
nourishing all around
its natural intelligence
always knowing

My Act of Forgiveness

I forgave myself for not being able to live up to the standards of perfection. Not only did I forgive myself, but I forgave everything and everyone, and every action, with my entire Being—including the center of my Being, my heart.

At that moment, I(My mind) suddenly became aware of my heart's essence, which felt like a glowing sensation in the region of the center of my chest. I had subconsciously been protecting my heart all my life.

Once again, I thought I had finally achieved "enlightenment"—and at that moment, the sunlight within me faded: I(My mind) had subconsciously shifted awareness from the region of my heart back to the region of my mind.

My mind now desired to recapture the state of awareness of my heart, which it had subconsciously lost. More subconscious self-created mental suffering would, therefore, continue.

I'm serious

Don't be so serious
It's all in your mind

My Mind Becomes Aware of the Voice from My Heart

I(My mind) eventually became so overcome with thoughts of suicide that I(My mind) lost awareness of nearly all of my surroundings. At this time, I(My mind) was somehow able to recall the teachings of the *Tao Te Ching* and *Hua Hu Ching* (see verses on page 40).

As I(My Being) lay on my bed, I(My mind) regained awareness of the energy within my heart. I(My mind) was able to quiet the suicidal voices enough to became aware of another voice, coming from my heart.

My mind thoroughly questioned the voice that was clearly coming from my heart:

Are you loving (asked my mind)?
   Yes (said my heart).

Are you virtuous (asked my mind)?
   Yes (said my heart).

Are you compassionate (asked my mind)?
   Yes (said my heart).

Are you forgiving (asked my mind)?
  Yes (said my heart).

Are you perfect (asked my mind)?
  No, since there cannot be perfect without imperfect (said my heart).

Who are you (asked my mind)?
  You and I are One (said my heart).

At this moment, I(My egoic self) surrendered all my previously acquired beliefs about myself and appointed the voice within my heart to be my teacher.

Over the many months to come, I(My mind) would learn from my new teacher—the voice coming from my heart, interpreted by my mind—that "I" had been a societally learned concept stored in my mind. "I" now knew itself as inseparable from "essence" of existence itself. Any separation between essence and myself had been my mind's own creation.

"My teachings are easy to understand
and easy to put into practice.

Yet your intellect will never grasp them,
and if you try to practice them, you'll fail.
My teachings are older than the world.
How can you grasp their meaning?

If you want to know me,
look inside your heart."

TAO TE CHING 70

"Do not go about worshipping deities
and religious institutions as the source of the
subtle truth. To do so is to place intermediaries
between yourself and the divine, and to make
of yourself a beggar who looks outside for
a treasure that is hidden inside his own breast.

If you want to worship the Tao,
first discover it in your own heart.
Then your worship will be meaningful."

HUA HU CHING 17

To think, or not to think;
that is the question

If I think I am an I, then I am an I

Am I an I?

My Ego Reasserts Itself

Having completely surrendered my egoic sense of self, I was left innocent and vulnerable (as a baby).

I(My mind) was frightened, since I had perceived at the time that I had completely given up my entire thought-based sense of identity.

I entered a state of complete depersonalization, in which I no longer recognized myself in the mirror. My mind desperately wanted to recover its former, well-defined egoic sense of self—it was too late. I had already completely accepted the voice within my mind, which had originated in my heart, as my teacher.

Any time I attempted to recover the recently surrendered thought-based sense of identity that I had identified with up until this point in my life, I endured immense mental suffering: the voices in my mind started to compete with each other (this is a mental state labeled "auditory hallucinations" in the *Diagnostic and Statistical Manual of Mental Disorders [DSM]*).

My mind had created its own life-or-death situation. This internal, vocally competing state quickly became too much for me (my mind-based sense of identity) to handle.

I had no choice but to stop listening to my former, egoic mind-based sense of self and to trust the one voice in my mind, which was originating from my heart.

mind vs heart

Unlike my mind, my heart never labels
or differentiates

My heart views its surroundings
as a Oneness bound together by love

My Cosmic Body

After quieting my mind's lifetime-acquired thoughts, I was able to reconnect with the original innocent voice from my heart. I(My mind) would go on to learn to know myself as not just a compilation of thoughts, but rather as a complete being.

"I" is simply a mind-constructed label.

This voice from my heart also taught me about my outer self—my cosmic or universal body—which I was seamlessly woven into.

It took months of self-exploration, and faith in the intelligence of my heart, to accept that I(My Being) am not a discreet entity.

I(My mind) came to the realization that the self (essence) and the cosmic self(essence) are I(1).

UnIverse

I was always there

My Search for I Has Ended

I(My mind) had been looking for answers that were always inside me.

The answer never left me.

The answer is love.

The answer was always in my heart.

I(essence) and the Universe(essence) are I(1).

universal heart of love

how beautiful is the heart when it is open
and free to sing its universal song of truth

bathed in a sea of sound and air swirling
around its life-giving force

in sync with the world around

giving and receiving all the love
it has always known

SECTION TWO

I AS
NON-DUAL I
(ONE)

The World of Non-Duality

It was the *Tao Te Ching* that introduced me to the concept of non-duality.

In the very first verse of the Tao, it is stated:

"The Tao that can be named is not the eternal Tao."

This simple yet profound statement describes the non-dual state.

Non-duality implies that, once you name or label the "thing," it is no longer the "thing" itself.

Non-Duality
as a State of Awareness

A human is aware of its existence through consciousness. Any mind-based attempt to observe or detect itself becomes a thought, name, label, symbol, representation, sensation, illusion, etc. of the self.

Therefore, like the Tao:

"The self that can be named (by the mind) is not the eternal self."

The Reductive (Dual) Nature of Labels and Symbols for "Things"

A name or label, or a symbol, can represent a "thing"; however, it cannot intrinsically be the "thing" itself. The "thing" is intrinsically itself.

I can say the word "apple," but only the apple itself can be the apple. No word, symbol, or number can be the actual "essence" or "energy form" that makes up an "apple." The name "apple" is arbitrary.

If I said "manzana," the Spanish word for "apple," and you did not understand Spanish, you would not be able to form your own image-creation of an apple in your mind.

The human mind creates an idea ("a mental quantum collapse") of "apple" by using its so-called five "physical" external senses (i.e., vision, taste, touch, smell, hearing) and its "non-physical" internal sense, known as thought.

These mind-created experiences brought about by the senses are heavily based on prior personal experiences. For example, a person who has only experienced small red apples in the past will always see a mental vision of a small red apple.

The actual essence of "apple" can never be intrinsically known. It can only be experienced, and known, in terms of our personal interaction with the unknown energy form "apple."

The Reductive (Dual) Nature of Labels and Symbols for "Humans"

In the same way, a name or label cannot intrinsically be the "Human" itself.

If the name "Human" is removed, the essence or intrinsic existence remains.

The term "Human" is itself reductive, since it is merely a scientifically agreed-upon name or label.

If the name "Human" is changed to "Coffee," or the newly created name "Widgety," its intrinsic nature or essence remains unchanged.

Although two "Humans" can share the name "Human," no two "Humans" are identical.

Not even "identical twins" are truly "identical."

Also, no matter how many named components are created for what makes up a "Human," i.e., "eyes, ears, nose, hair, blood, water, serotonin, American, Jewish, bipolar, schizophrenic, electron, neutrino, etc.," the intrinsic existence of the named "Human" cannot be recreated by these names.

"Human" intrinsic existence came long before language evolved.

"Human" intrinsic existence just is.

There are no words for this.

The Observable (and Non-Observable) Universe as a Reflection of Ourselves

What we observe when we look at the sky and heavens are the very limitations of our own perceptions.

If we were blind, we would see nothing. If we could see all parts of the electromagnetic spectrum, we would be blinded by light. If we could hear all frequencies and amplitudes of sound, our ears would be deafened by noise.

It is not possible to know the true identity of "reality (intrinsic existence, essence)" because of the limitations of human perception, and also because humans are a part of the very essence itself. Once "reality" is perceived by the mind, it is no longer "reality," but is now reduced to a "named thought-based perception of reality."

Perception can be agreed upon collectively by a group of people called "scientists."

In the past, based on the observations and beliefs of scientists (specifically, astronomers), the Earth was believed to be at the center of the Universe (the geocentric model).

The Earth was once also believed to be flat.

Societal perceptions change over time. Changes are based largely upon the collective belief system of the culture.

Science as the Creation of Dualities

A duality is the mental formation (individual or collective) of a discreet entity from intrinsic existence.

Humans create dualities (usually by utilizing vision sense) by naming, labeling, and numbering things that have an intrinsic existence.

The already-named or soon-to-be-named essence is either already within our limited "intrinsic detector" vision sense, or is brought into our vision sense by the use of an external detector device.

The "observer human," named "scientist," and what is being observed—"another human or non-human"—can never be in isolation from each other. When the actual essence is detected, both the scientist(essence) and that which is observed(essence) are changed during the very act of detection. In this way, the essence itself can never be known in its intrinsic form.

Thought and Sense Perceptions Creating Dualities

The scientist-named "Earth" was formed by accretion from the nebula of the scientist-named "Sun." These "two" entangled energy systems, called "Sun" and "Earth" (or, alternatively, a single "Sun-Earth system") have been, are currently, and always will be in continuous connection. They are also in continuous flux, continuously exchanging energy with each other. Any boundaries that have been created have been formally agreed upon by the collective consciousness in the minds of scientists over the ages.

Humanity has traditionally placed a high value on its visual senses. Therefore, most named things are based on the requirement for a photoelectric coupling, which enables the "eye" detector of a human to observe an event. The naming of "things" as being different from other "things" is predominately on the basis of differences in the photoelectric couplings.

This is why we have one name for "space" and another name for "atmosphere." In "space," there are fewer photoelectric couplings (and, thus, we perceive space as darker, since we rely on photoelectric couplings to see) than there are in the "atmosphere."

Similarly, if an object with enough photoelectric couplings for our visual perception behaves in a manner that is outside the realm of our prior cosmological observational experience, a scientific deduction is made that there must be another object present that is below our limited visual perception. A new name is then assigned to this low photoelectric coupling object (i.e., dark energy, dark matter, black hole, etc.).

Scientific Proof
We and the Universe Are One

According to modern observational cosmology, named "Humans" and the named "Universe" were both born from a named "Big Bang."

Although acquiring the name "Human" is usually based upon the perceived boundary of the body within the visible light spectrum, Humans can also be detected in the microwave portion of the electromagnetic spectrum.

When the cosmic microwave radiation is measured, We (as named "Humans") are a part of this measurement, since we are woven into the Universe.

When a measurement for the age of the Universe (which includes the Human form) is taken, it is the self-aware Universe measuring itself.

DEFINITIONS

Big Bang—The prevailing cosmological theory that the entirety of the Universe arose from an initial high thermal energy contracted state into its current cooling, expanding state.

Cosmic Microwave Background (CMB)—The CMB is the detected thermal radiation left over from the theorized Big Bang.

True Self as the Non-Dual State of Self

The true self is the non-dual state of self. This true self is not a self at all, because "self" is simply a mind-assigned label.

The true non-dual self is, therefore, an indescribable, unnamable entity that can only be referred to by a similar analogy, which I have used in previous references: I am an unknowable energy form that is blended into the over-all energy forms comprising the entirety of all energy forms (the so-called named "Universe").

Ego as the Dual State of Self

The egoic self is a mind-based, thought-created sense of self and, therefore, is merely a representation of a self. This thought-form sense of self considers itself to be separate from the Universe.

For example, my egoic self tried to assert itself as its own separate entity. Its mind believed itself as self because this self had acquired a name (Jeffrey), and It was assigned a named species (Homo sapiens), which enabled It to talk to itself in the context that included other names, labels, and symbols (I, me, we, etc.)

However, just as with science, nothing (including myself) was ever created or discovered. I(My mind) acquired a name and a belief system, but the I(My Being) was always just an unnamable and unknowable energy form in flux, inseparable from the entirety of all energy forms called Universe.

Subtle and Non-Subtle Forms of a "Tornado"

Scientists decided to name "tornado," as well as name the requirements that would fit the definition (i.e., the wind speed, visual appearance, etc., relative to us) of the form, "tornado."

Even though "tornado" and "atmosphere" have different names, a "tornado" is always completely inseparable from "atmosphere." As the "tornado" starts to take form from the "atmosphere," it remains unnamed (but still in existence) until it meets the requirements for the agreed-upon scientific definition. When the "tornado" meets the requirements for its definition, it acquires the name "tornado." When it loses the requirements to fit the definition, the name "tornado" is no longer applied to this area of the atmosphere. However, even unnamed, its existence remains.

Throughout both its named and unnamed existence, it has always been continuously connected and exchanging energy with its surroundings. It has always been in continuous flux.

Subtle and Non-Subtle Forms of "I" Myself

As with the tornado, so it was with me. I acquired the name "Jeffrey" when I took form relative to the observation of my parents, at my birth. Prior to exiting the womb, I had existed in different energy states and, since then, I have been constantly changing form, as I live. By convention, my name remains "Jeffrey" throughout my lifetime. I will become less and less formed as "Jeffrey" until the eventual cessation of myself as "Human" form, at which time a new form will come into existence.

Throughout my existence in "Human" form, I have been continuously connected and exchanging energy with my surroundings (light, air, water, etc.). I am always in continuous flux. There are never discreet boundaries between me and my surroundings. It is the different names of "things" that provoke the mental illusion of separation.

Knowledge of Self Through Consciousness

My true self can never know itself by observation. When looking at myself in the mirror, I am not seeing myself, but only a reflection of myself. I am seeing a visual manifestation of a self, which requires additional photo-electric couplings for the sensation of vision to occur. That is not who I am. When I close my eyes, I disappear from a visual perspective.

The non-dual true self is aware of its existence because it is conscious.

Since I am seamlessly woven into the Universe, the Universe itself is conscious.

Ego as the Creation of a Self by Thought-Observation

It was my mind-based ego's quest to define my existence as something other than the Universe that I am woven into. This caused the immense mental suffering I endured.

Thought, like any other sense, is a reductive re-creation of my identity.

The egoic self is a thought-based reductive sense of self.

A thought of self is not a self. It is only a representation, symbol, or illusion of self.

For this reason, any time I(My mind) thought of myself as separate from the Universe, or any time I(My mind) tried to figure out who I(My Being, or essence, which is intrinsically unknowable by my mind) was, I(My mind) created its own suffering.

Life is a divine comedy!

The Scientific Dualistic Perception of the Universe

The agreed-upon perception of the Universe by science is "dualistic" since it is based upon a consensus of thought that "We" (the observer) are separate from the "Universe" (the observed). This has led to our minds' naming of different "things."

For example, the geocentric view placed our own named "selves" on our own named "Earth" within the center of our own named "Universe."

This theory was later replaced by a heliocentric view, which places our own named "Sun" in the center of our own named "solar system."

As mind-based scientific thought progressed, we began to place our own named "Sun" near the periphery of our own named "Milky Way" galaxy.

The Rise of the Non-Dual Universe Becoming Aware of Its Consciousness

The next natural step would be the evolution of our understanding of the Universe as from "dualistic" to "non-dualistic," with the cessation of separation between the mental concept of "We" and "Universe."

Since "We" are aware of our own consciousness, and "We" are inseparable from the "Universe," the "Universe" itself is becoming aware that it is conscious.

We are the Universe gazing back at itself.

The Universe is observing itself through "Us."

We are the eyes of the Universe.

We and the Universe are quantumly entangled.

We and the Universe are I(one).